Tessa bought a yo-yo.
Tessa went to school with her yo-yo.

Tessa wanted to do tricks with her yo-yo.
Her friends wanted to do tricks too.

2

'This is hard,' said Jamila.
'Could I have a go?' said Rocky.
He had a go with the yo-yo.
'It is hard,' he said.

Kevin wanted to have a go.
He grabbed the yo-yo.

Kevin dropped the yo-yo.
He was cross.
'This is too hard!' he said.

Tessa went into class with her yo-yo.
Mr Belter said, 'Have you got a yo-yo, Tessa?'
'Yes,' said Tessa.

Mr Belter wanted the yo-yo.
Tessa gave her teacher the yo-yo.

'Look at Mr Belter,' said Tessa.
The children looked.

Mr Belter made the yo-yo go up and down, up and down.

He did tricks with the yo-yo.
They were good tricks, too!

Tessa and her friends talked to the teacher.
After school, Mr Belter gave the children a
yo-yo class.

'It is not too hard!' said Kevin.